An Ordinary Life

With Extraordinary Moments

K.C.Bernard

Table of Contents

To my husband Mark, for his unwavering belief in

me then, and now

About the Author

I have known for a very long time that I needed to write my story. The knowing changed in intensity over the years, and if I was lucky, I was able to keep myself so busy that I would forget about it for lengthy periods of time. The knowing remained.

Whenever I took time to think about putting words on paper, I found myself in such uncertainty – where to start, what, and how much to write – I would end up just putting the idea back on the shelf.

A part of me was excited to sit down and simply write the words; after all, I love words and believe they have such power when used intentionally. Another part, perhaps the greater part, was terrified. I would be exposing the deepest, most vulnerable part of myself to others. What if the work wasn't well received? What if it made no impact? What if I failed?

The knowing persisted, along with several other factors. I began to facilitate groups for sexual abuse survivors, and I saw first-hand the profound impact made when one survivor shared their story with the others in the room. I have witnessed the healing that happens when a voice that has been silenced for a lifetime finds the courage to express itself.

It is an awe-inspiring experience.

My own healing journey was possible because I was graced with a small circle of guardian angels in the form of family, of blood and of heart, who encouraged me, stood by me, protected me, and ultimately created a safe space for me to speak what had been silenced for too long.

I now know the power of the story, my story. It is filled with the hard and the dark, the bright and the joyful. It speaks to the ordinary and the extraordinary of life, and it is mine to speak, mine to share.

I believe it is a strong story, one that is woven throughout with the unbreakable thread of faith – my faith in a loving God who wept when I did, who held me when I was in despair, and who showered me with love when I found my way out of the dark and into the light.

And so, I step out on the ledge, my story in your hands, hoping that somewhere in these pages, a word, a phrase, a thought, a feeling, finds its way to your heart. That single moment connects us.

Thank you for reading my story; for doing so, you give witness to my truth, my voice, and my healing. I am grateful!

Chapter 1

Growing Up...

I was born on an island in the Caribbean to a large family, the fifth of eight children. My mother was an only child and came from a privileged background. She was spoiled and sheltered. My father came from a large family and had to learn how to fend for himself. They married when my mom was twenty-one and my dad twenty-eight.

My dad was a fun parent. He laughed easily, took us on beach vacations, loved having house parties, and generally enjoyed a good time with friends, food, and drink.

While he was the more fun-loving, he also had a quick temper and had no concept of faithfulness to his marriage vows. There was a steady stream of mistresses during my childhood, and my mother knew about all of them.

Our family life had moments of fun and lightheartedness; and silent, brittle moments where neither parent spoke to the other. We would go from playing happily outside to huddling together, hiding from them as they lashed out at each other.

Inevitably, my mother would reach a breaking point and pack her bags to leave. She never did. She would quiz us, "Who would you want to be with if I ever left your dad?" We would tearfully answer, "You, Mommy."

That seemed to satisfy her.

For the first five years, I was a happy child. I loved singing, dancing, and showing off any new dresses that I owned. As a pre-schooler, I would sometimes put on one of those dresses and stand at the end of our driveway when I knew the school children were heading home just so they could pass by and see my beautiful dress. I believed I was very special and wasn't shy about showing the world how amazing I was.

Chapter 2

As a child growing up on the islands, life was simple. We went to school, did our homework, and played. Having such a large family meant there was always someone to play with, and the tropical weather meant we could spend hours outdoors, creating new games and adventures. Other times we were inside, playing 'beauty pageant.' We would raid my mom's closet and model her clothes, her shoes, and whatever we could find. My brother, Ryan, was always the judge, and he learned very quickly that choosing one sister over the others didn't bode well for him. We created the only pageant where everyone was a winner!

One of my favorite childhood memories is the beach outings we enjoyed. My parents would allow us to sleep in our bathing suits the night before so we wouldn't waste time getting ready in the morning. The adults would wake before dawn to cook for the whole day. The drive seemed endless, and then finally, we'd arrive, and the day would be spent in and out of the water, eating from the pots in the trunk of our car and drinking coconut water from the coconuts my dad would shake off the trees. Carefree and happy!

Life changed for me at the age of five, and by the time I was seven, my marks at school began to suffer. I developed stomach pains, and my parents took me to various doctors. Test after test followed, including regular blood tests.

I looked forward to those trips to the clinic because I got to have more time alone with my mom, and I could believe for a little while that she wanted to take care of me. I cherished those times with her because, even as a child, I had always felt that she didn't love me. She seemed harsher with me than with the other siblings and was quicker to get angry with me. I never knew why.

No definitive diagnosis was ever made from the result of those tests. There was talk of exploratory surgery; fortunately, our papers came through for immigrating to Canada, and our family doctor suggested that Canada had more medical resources, and he recommended waiting. Thankfully, my parents agreed.

Coming to Canada was a traumatic experience. It meant leaving our relatives, our friends, and our classmates. It meant having to say goodbye to everything familiar and dear.

My father came first to secure a job and housing. Through loose connections, he was able to stay in the basement of a family who originally came from our homeland and had settled in Toronto years earlier. What a culture shock for my dad! His phone calls home were filled with stories of the strange things he saw while traveling the subway to job interviews. He was scandalized by the sight of men and women wearing their underwear in public. In truth, they were wearing tank tops, something that was completely foreign to him.

It wasn't long before my father became homesick and wanted to return home. A desperate phone call to my mother, telling her he was coming back, had my mother making immediate plans to join him.

Within a week, my mother had arranged to have the eight of us farmed out to various relatives and friends and was on a flight to Toronto. Nothing was going to stop her from starting a new life in Canada.

We spent almost a month without our parents, and finally, the day came for us to leave. My memories of that morning are blurred, but I do recall the busyness of getting ready, food being prepared, and nerves, lots of nerves.

Once we arrived at the airport, we were surrounded by relatives and friends, many with tears streaming down their faces. The goodbyes were heart-wrenching, and then the moment came when we had to climb the steps leading to the departure lounge; eight children ranging from four years of age to fifteen, leaving behind everyone and everything we had ever known.

I remember bits and pieces of our flight to Montreal and then boarding a connecting flight to Toronto. Mixed in with all those nerves was excitement over our first plane ride and reuniting with our parents.

Another clear memory is standing at Arrivals in the Toronto airport and hearing my dad's name being paged. As we stood huddled in a group, we saw our dad rushing to the escalators and getting on one going in the wrong direction, then rushing back down and finally reaching us. Our mom was steps behind him. A joyful reunion!

As we began the process of settling in, I found myself missing my home, the familiar surroundings and way of life, and my friends. At almost ten, I was old enough to know what I was missing, yet too young to really understand all the changes. Our new neighborhood consisted of only white families, and as a family of color, we were viewed with suspicion and dislike. Some residents sold their homes and moved away, believing that we would bring down property values by moving into the neighborhood.

Those early years in Canada were fraught with homesickness, the anxiety of not fitting in, and being painfully aware of our Caribbean accent, our brown skin color, and the size of our family. We endured racial slurs, uneducated assumptions, and overt hostility. Despite those hardships, my father would drum into us that we had to work twice as hard at school so that Canada would never regret its decision to allow us into the country.

Looking back, I believe my mother was the one who pushed my father to move to Canada, and I'll never really know, but I suspect she hoped that their marriage would get back on track and my father would give up his adulterous ways.

That didn't happen.

It didn't take long for the same pattern to resurface, and the eight of us were subjected, once again, to the; "Whose side would you take?" question from our mother.

A different country, same story.

As children, we knew how to make our own fun. Since we had moved during the summer, school was weeks away. We sat in awe in front of the television. So many channels! Back home, we used to wait eagerly every Saturday evening for the television signal to come on at 5:00 PM – one channel, only on the weekend, only in the evening. We discovered popsicles and how to break them apart against a hard surface. I made the delicious acquaintance of Sweet Marie – a chocolate bar, unlike anything I'd ever known.

One of my older sisters formed a deep attachment to the toaster – for us, a new and wonderful appliance. She could and would eat toast at any given time of the day. We marveled at everything - from ice-cream sandwiches to cream-filled donuts; from multi-colored marshmallows to pink lemonade – we were in heaven!

Eventually, we settled into a rhythm. My father continued having affairs; my mother still threatened to leave him; we went to school, made friends, and joined teams.

In the early years of our life in Canada, we connected with other families from 'back home,' and summers would find us organizing multi-family picnics that had as many as thirty people attending. Each family would bring their own food – cooked early that morning – and the day would be spent playing sports, swimming, eating, and simply enjoying being in the company of people who looked and talked like us.

To this day, as I walk through our neighborhood park, I see new Canadians repeating those very same rituals. It's the immigrant way.

Our home was always open to friends. If we asked if a friend could stay for dinner, my father would say, "What's one more?" He encouraged us to have our friends over. He would say, "At least I'll know who you're with and where you are."

There were many challenges to being part of such a big family! Lack of privacy, waiting in line to use the bathroom, noise, tripping over shoes at the front door, not enough closet space…the list was endless!

Christmas was the biggest exception. I loved our home at Christmas! Having my birthday three days before

Christmas added another level of excitement. On Christmas Eve, we'd put on our new Christmas nightgowns or pajamas and sit around the coffee table, which was laden with bite-sized morsels of spicy roast pork and homemade bread. This had been our traditional Christmas Eve dinner for as long as I can remember; one that crossed over into Canada and one that we kids loved.

Late in the evening, we'd walk to church for Midnight Mass. As a child, there was something magical about being out so late at night with the whole family. Snow added its own magic. After Mass, the question would be asked repeatedly, "Do you think Santa has already arrived?" We'd race home, only to find he hadn't.

Once home, there'd be a flurry of activity to haul pillows and blankets down to the basement, where we'd set up makeshift beds so that we could all be together. Our excitement couldn't be contained, and my dad would have to come down and warn us that Santa wouldn't come if we were still awake. That always had the desired effect. Cherished memories!

My parents enjoyed having house parties, and our home would be party central for their friends, as my parents had quickly connected with others who had emigrated from our homeland. While I enjoyed the music, the dancing, and the food, I hated when the evening wore on, and my parents' friends would become drunk. Inevitably, it meant some of the men would find a way to get my sisters or me in a corner and kiss us. At twelve, I was embarrassed, ashamed, and disgusted.

I never told anyone.

I did have a terrible crush on one of my parents' friends. He was much younger than my parents, was married, and had two small children. He was fun and always paid a lot of attention to me. At twelve, I was painfully shy and always felt like an ugly duckling. I reveled in his attention and was completely infatuated.

I remember the first time I had to stay at home from school because I was sick. My mother asked my 'uncle' to check in on me because he worked shifts and was home during the day. He made me something to eat, then sat with me and hugged me. The next day, he came again and, this time, he kissed me. I never liked those kisses, but I craved the attention, and it wasn't long before my twelve-year-old romantic heart was in love. My 'uncle' found ways to get me alone, and if there was anything more than those kisses, I don't remember.

As abruptly as it had begun, it stopped, and I felt abandoned and ashamed. It never once occurred to me that my 'uncle' was in the wrong. I was the one who carried the shame.

The summer I was fourteen, I remember being in the kitchen with two of my older sisters. We were reminiscing about our childhood, and one of them casually asked, "Do you guys remember Joe?"

Joe was a friend of my parents who babysat us when my parents went out for the evening. I did remember Joe because my very first memory as a small child – two or three years of age – was of Joe putting my hand on his penis.

For the first time, I shared that memory with my sisters. They laughed and said the same thing had happened to them, and then we all laughed. My mother came into the kitchen and asked what we were laughing about. We told her, and she was shocked.

It never occurred to us that what Joe did wasn't a laughing matter, and we never talked about it again.

Chapter 3

On the home front, life continued to offer the fun and the fractious. My brother Ryan and I were in the same grade and shared common friends. Our high school years revolved around basketball games, house parties, and the drama of requited and unrequited love. Summers were spent at jobs, earning money for university, and weekend trips to the beach.

I excelled in high school, had good friends, and loved a boy who loved me back for a short while, and then he didn't. I was devastated when he broke up with me because he was the first person who had ever told me that he loved me. I'd never heard those words before from anyone, including my parents.

My parents' marriage continued to be dysfunctional. There were times when my mother would ask Darlene's boyfriend to drive to my father's workplace to see if his car was still in the parking lot. My father would have told my mother he'd be working late, but she had good reason to be suspicious. Inevitably, his car would be gone, and we knew what that meant.

At seventeen, I started my first year at university, and I fell apart. I was without my high school friends and lonely. My father was having yet another affair, and my mother was an angry and emotional wreck...again. I couldn't concentrate, and I felt myself slowly sinking into the quicksand of our dysfunctional life.

In the following years, I stumbled in and out of university life. I couldn't function. I began to have breathing problems. Just like my stomach ache, and despite numerous tests, no diagnosis was made.

I was sent to a psychologist, who tried her best to teach me relaxation techniques. I tried to self-hypnotize, as she suggested, by imagining steps and going up each step, one by one, and breathing. I really didn't understand. I still don't.

What did steps have to do with the feeling I had that I was dying?

When I got off the bus near my house at the end of the school day, I'd struggle to breathe. I felt my father's disappointment in my academic disaster keenly. He couldn't understand. I'd been a straight-A student in high school, editor of the school yearbook, and recipient of the language award as well as a provincial scholarship. My name was on a plaque at my high school.

What was wrong with me?

At twenty, I began to date a friend of my younger brother. Mark had been trying for over a year to get me to go out with him. He was almost two years younger than I was, and I hadn't taken him seriously. Finally, his persistence paid off, and we began to date.

At twenty-one, I jumped at the chance to share a basement apartment with a friend. I switched to being a part-time student and increased my hours working at a part-time job. The day I moved out, Mark came to pick me up with his station wagon. I had my clothes in a bag, a few trinkets, and $200 my mother gave me.

My father told me that leaving home without getting married meant that I would have a revolving front door for boys. Later that week, my father passed out in the bathroom. My oldest sister called me, screaming that I was trying to kill him.

My father didn't speak to me for a year and a half.

Moving out saved my life and, more importantly, my sanity. While I missed my brothers and sisters, I felt the joy of freedom, freedom from the tumultuous roller coaster ride that was my family.

After that first year with a roommate, I made the decision to drop out of university, get a full-time job, and move into my very own apartment. It was a painful decision and a radical one in the eyes of my father. He had expectations of me, and I was choosing not to live up to them.

To this day, I don't know how I found the courage or the determination to take those life-altering steps away from my father's vision for my life. As the middle child in my family, I had always tried my best not to make waves. I was the one my siblings (mostly my brothers) would turn to for a loan or a favor. I was the one my friends turned to for advice. I was the pleaser.

Having my own place, something that belonged to me alone, was a miracle. I'd never been happier. For the very first time in my life, I felt I had the space to breathe. It was intoxicating.

Time mellowed my father, and he finally accepted the reality of my independence. Getting engaged to Mark also made both him and my mother very happy. My parents loved him, possibly more than they had ever loved me.

I used to say that if Mark ever ran me down in the streets, my mother would conclude that he'd had a hard day at work and make him a meal while I lay bleeding on the road. Dramatic…maybe!

My younger brother Dean got engaged to a girl he'd met at university. Her family still lived in the Caribbean, and the wedding was going to take place there.

Weeks before we were scheduled to attend the wedding, I began to experience severe abdominal pain. The pain was so debilitating that I couldn't stand up straight. Thankfully, it was sporadic, and I was able to join my family as we traveled for my brother's wedding. It was the first time that all of us (minus my sisters Darlene and Sara) would be returning to our homeland, my parents included.

When I returned to Canada, it was almost Christmas, and I was too busy to pay attention to the pain that had returned almost daily. I ignored it and kept on going. By January of the New Year, I couldn't ignore it any longer. That entire year was a blur of tests, procedures, hospital stays, and antibiotics, with no real diagnosis.

It was such a stressful time for Mark and me. We'd only been married for two years, and Mark was working full-time and taking university courses in the evenings. During my hospital stays, he'd come to visit and bring his books to study. It certainly wasn't what either of us had signed on for.

The following year, I was referred to a new family doctor. He was a medical doctor, but he also believed in alternative approaches, like naturopathy and homeopathy. I learned a great deal from him. He was a tall, handsome man with kind eyes, a gentle smile, and a compassionate heart.

After two years of trying various treatments, the pain continued. My doctor suggested I see a craniosacral massage therapist. I had no idea what that was and was reluctant. The pain won out, however, and I booked an appointment, trusting that my doctor knew what he was doing.

I didn't know what to expect the first time I arrived for my appointment. I expected to meet a clinical, impersonal therapist, and instead, I met Alice. She was warm and kind, and she put me at ease. It turns out craniosacral massage doesn't have anything to do with vigorous manipulation of my head (my assumption); and everything to do with a gentle, healing touch. There's a lot of science to back up this type of massage; all I knew was it was relaxing and easy and had profound results.

This feels nice, but I don't see how it's going to help me, I thought to myself.

As Alice was gently working on my body, she began to quietly speak about some of her female patients who had similar abdominal pain that was a result of personal trauma. She believed that they held their pain in their bodies.

The words felt like knives in my heart, and I began to cry; right there on the massage table, in the presence of someone I'd only just met. Alice said nothing about my tears, finished our session, and with infinitely wise eyes, gently said, "You may want to speak to someone about this."

She gave me the name of two psychotherapists she knew personally, and I left.

I ignored those names for a little while, but they nagged at me, taunting me. As hard as I tried, I couldn't forget the feeling of utter desolation I'd experienced, lying on that massage table, hearing the word "trauma."

I chose one of those two therapists and made an appointment. Kate made me nervous, and I went home after our first session, declaring to my husband that I didn't like her and that I wasn't going to book a second session. When he asked me why I didn't like her, I replied, "She has cat's eyes, and I feel as if she can see right through me."

I made another appointment.

On the home front, Mark and I were happily married. I had found a part-time job and felt good about contributing to our expenses. I was still closely connected to my parents and my siblings and tried my best to be a good daughter and sister. It never seemed to be enough.

After a particularly tumultuous family argument over - believe it or not - my father's retirement party, I realized, in one of those profound moments of clarity, that nothing I ever did would be enough to earn my mother's approval.

God knows I'd tried!

I began to distance myself from my family. My sessions with Kate were enlightening. She was a gentle listener, and I found myself exploring the family dynamics that were so obviously severely dysfunctional.

Yet another argument, one with my brother Dean led to the beginning of a journey that upended my life.

Dean had come over to confront me over some imagined slight against his wife. He was angry, and the louder he became, the smaller I felt. Abruptly, I left the room and ran up to the bedroom, where I huddled in the corner, with my hands over my ears, rocking back and forth, whispering, "I hate the yelling!"

Dean was shocked into silence, and Mark was terrified. Once we were alone, he immediately called Kate, and she explained to him that I was experiencing a type of regression brought on by my brother's yelling. She asked Mark to ask me how old I was – my answer was five.

She then encouraged him to speak to me as if I were indeed five. Surprisingly, he did so easily, and it didn't take long for me to return to myself. I was aware that my 'adult self' had never left. It was as if the five-year-old me was driving the car and my 'adult self' was in the back seat.

From that moment on, my life was a roller-coaster of events. I believe the combination of family arguments and my time spent in therapy led to cracks in the wall I had built around deep-seated trauma that had taken place throughout my childhood.

That initial regression opened the door for endless others. In the beginning, they centered on all the fighting that had taken place between my parents and my feelings of fear and anxiety.

And then my world crashed.

Throughout my childhood and into adulthood, I'd carried a few 'snapshots' of memories that were deeply troubling. The first one was of me at around age seven, standing in a room in our home, silently screaming in my head. The second was being in Canada, lying in bed at night and being terrified to move, knowing my dad was standing at the doorway, and finally, the last and most disturbing was a memory of my father, naked.

While I had begun to accept the regressions as part of my healing, I was blindsided by the one from that five-year-old that revealed her overwhelming pain, fear, and confusion at being sexually assaulted by her dad.

Those memories hurtled me into the abyss.

I shared the details of my experiences with only one sister. Sara and I had always been close, more like kindred spirits. She was quirky and fun, and I laughed more easily when I was with her. As the memories invaded, I would look to her to confirm what I was remembering. While she had no memory of the actual abuse, she could confirm the details I provided of certain rooms in our old house as well as certain family situations. She became a lifeline for me.

Mark and I were elated to find out we were having our first child. I fervently hoped that the memories would stop and I could concentrate on being pregnant and readying our home for the baby. That didn't happen. In fact, the memories only intensified.

I remember asking my family doctor if our baby would be harmed by all the tears and the suffering. He said, "You're doing all you can to uncover the truth; how could that possibly harm your child?"

His response was exactly the reassurance I needed.

At eight months pregnant, I sat in the doctor's office with painful blisters on the back of my neck. My doctor took one look, shook his head, and sighed, "You have shingles." What followed was three weeks of agonizing pain and very little sleep.

I had barely begun to rebound from shingles when I went into labor. Twenty-four hours later and beyond exhaustion, our baby entered the world.

Life became even more complicated with the birth of our son, Michael. He was the first grandson of my parents, which meant frequent visits. I was trying to deal with the trauma of remembering my father had sexually abused me while maintaining a relationship with my parents.

The stress was overwhelming!

Chapter 4

My journey of being a mom began, and I enjoyed every bit of it. I continued my work with Kate, learned how to be a mom, and feigned a relationship with my parents. I knew I couldn't keep up the pretense for much longer, yet I couldn't take that next step of either confronting my father or simply walking away.

At a routine chiropractic appointment, my chiropractor noticed that both of my arms were quite swollen. He expressed concern and strongly recommended that I see my family doctor to be tested for rheumatoid arthritis.

I immediately dismissed his concerns, attributing it to the number of times I picked up my one-year-old, but the seed had been planted. After a few months, I booked an appointment, had blood work taken, and fully expected good news.

There's reason to panic when you get a phone call from your family doctor at 11 pm on a Friday night. The news wasn't good. My blood work was positive for rheumatoid arthritis with factors linked to systemic lupus.

I couldn't believe that, after all, I'd been going through, all the pain and heartache of remembering my trauma, of having to relive it in order to let it go, I was now going to have to fight again, this time, for my physical health.

Immediately, there was a flurry of appointments with my family doctor and a rheumatologist. I was x-rayed from head to toe. As I lay on that cold, hard x-ray table, I experienced a surge of rage. I remember thinking that this illness was a direct result of my father's abuse. How horribly perfect to be diagnosed with an autoimmune illness that didn't recognize the difference between friend or foe … *The story of my life!*

After all the testing and x-rays, I met with my rheumatologist, who outlined his treatment plan for me. It included medication that came with the possibility of such terrifying side effects, and I said 'no' to all of them. I'm so grateful to my husband for supporting that decision, with the understanding that if my illness progressed, I would revisit the decision. I agreed.

For three years, I made regular appointments with my rheumatologist and had blood work taken. I stopped those appointments after he advised me against trying to have a second child. He spoke of the possibility of 'spontaneous termination' and 'inability to go to the term.'

I thanked him for all his efforts and left his office. I never returned. I was determined to heal from my emotional trauma with the hope that it would benefit my physical health and I was also determined to have a second child.

My emotional healing took a giant leap at, of all places, a sandbox. I had taken Michael to a park that held a giant sandbox. At two years of age, he was obsessed with construction vehicles, so we packed up some of his trucks, and off we went for a morning of play. It didn't take long for another child to look enviously at Michael's toy, toddle over and take it.

Michael looked at me, lips trembling, trusting me to make things right. Pushing through my intense fear of confrontation, I walked over to the child's mother and asked to have the toy returned. It was the first time I'd used my voice to advocate for my child, something I'd never done for myself, and it awakened in me a fierce protector.

Enter my sister, Karen.

I knew that my younger sister had also been seeing a therapist to deal with her own trauma at the hands of our father. Unlike me, she had no problem deciding to confront him and had told Sara and me that she planned on doing so when she was ready.

Late one night, Mark and I were in bed sleeping when there was a loud knock on the door. We stumbled out of bed to find my brother Dean at the door. He'd come to drive me to our parents' home. The entire family was gathering because earlier that day, my sister Karen had confronted my father, accusing him of molesting her, and had declared she wanted nothing to do with him or my mother, whom she felt had done nothing to keep Karen safe.

I was stunned and terrified. I told him I'd drive myself over, and after he left, I quickly called my sister Sara, who was also on her way to our parents' home. She, too, had been summoned to the family home.

Once there, we listened, hearts banging inside our chests, to what had transpired that day. Karen had come to the house, raged at our father, accused him of molesting her, and raged at our mother for knowing and doing nothing to stop him.

The atmosphere in the house was one I knew only too well. We were in lockdown crisis mode. Everyone was on high alert. This couldn't happen to our family. My siblings were outraged on my parents' behalf. Everyone talked at once, with the rallying cry of "We need to stand together!"

My father was calm and collected. He loved nothing better than this – having his children rally around him, their loyalty loudly proclaimed. Karen was the traitor, the one who had broken rank and had deserted the family. She was now excommunicated from our family and stripped of all rights and privileges that came with being a family member.

While this loud, belligerent conversation was taking place, Sara and I were hiding in the kitchen under the pretense of making tea. We couldn't say anything and decided to meet at a nearby coffee shop once the gathering began to break up.

It was evident to all that we were not eager to denounce Karen, and eyebrows were raised at our reluctance. We claimed that shock had rendered us speechless, and that seemed to satisfy the room.

As we parked behind the neighborhood coffee shop, now well into the night, Sara and I were freaked out. How did we deal with this? Did we say that we knew about Karen's intention? Did I reveal my own trauma? Did I reach out to the siblings? To my parents?

We parted ways, still in a full-blown panic.

After two days of fearful and frantic conversations with Mark and Sara, I decided I had to step up and stand by Karen. The feeling that she had forced my hand was overshadowed by my unwillingness to let her stand alone.

I called a siblings' meeting. All came, except for Karen and my sister Darlene in the U.S. I shared with them my own story, my own experience of being molested by our father. It was one of the hardest things I've ever done, and it left me vulnerable and scared.

I had always believed that my siblings and I were a close, tight-knit group. We had huddled together throughout the stormy years of our parents' dysfunctional marriage. We had cried together, laughed together, and grown-up together.

This moment would either confirm that belief or shatter it. As they got up one by one and walked out, I found myself looking only at Mark and Sara. The others had taken a stand, and it wasn't with me. They were clear – our parents were the priority. There was no discussion as to whether the accusations were true; it didn't even seem to matter. (Darlene would tell me many years later that she had to choose between our mom and me. She didn't choose me.)

A line had been drawn, and Karen and I were on one side, with five siblings on the other. Sara would join us soon after, as she was asked to meet with our father. After hearing of my meeting with my siblings, my dad had met with them and insisted that they choose sides. They already had. Sara declared her support for me and was immediately told to leave both home and family.

I will always be indebted to her for her belief in me.

From that moment on, my life was divided into the time before and the time after that day.

It didn't take my father long – a matter of weeks – to join a support group for victims of 'False Memory Syndrome.' The group's members were comprised of people who insisted they were falsely accused of sexual abuse. My father was now on a mission. He arrived at Mark's workplace armed with a folder of literature on FMS, intent on proving to Mark that I had been brainwashed by my therapist.

The irony was that Kate had been offered an opportunity to start her own retreat out of the country at the beginning of the year and I was no longer seeing her. That significant detail had no impact on my father.

The separation was a painful yet liberating experience. While I grieved the loss of my family and our many traditions, I was finally free to explore my own healing, create a nurturing home for my family and re-define 'family' with my two sisters.

It was far from perfect.

While Sara and I had always been close, Karen had been more aligned with siblings on the other side of the line. We were now thrown together, and her discomfort was evident; however, we were determined and desperate to create a sense of family for our children. Every so often, Karen would take issue with something Sara and I did and would 'opt out of our lives, taking her kids with her. A year (sometimes two or three) later, she would re-enter. While our kids felt the loss of their cousins keenly, it too became familiar. They found comfort in Sara's consistent love and the fun they enjoyed with her three daughters.

My own healing felt complete. I became stronger, more confident, and filled with an inner strength that allowed me to explore my own interests. I loved being a mother and found the nurturing of my children to be especially healing. Loving and caring for them felt like loving and caring for myself. I discovered a passion for local and global outreach and became involved in several programs through the school and church community. I felt whole.

It had been a year since the family split, and our own little family of three had just returned from a Florida vacation. Michael had loved walking on the beach, collecting shells, and playing in the water. I thought of all that my parents were missing and, once back home, I summoned up my courage and called my mother, asking if she wanted to have a visit with Michael. (I didn't have the emotional strength to include my father) It was the first call I'd made to her in a year.

We arranged to meet at a local café, my mother, Michael, and myself. My mother was delighted to spend time with Michael, and no mention of the family split was made. Finally, it was time to leave. I offered my mother the chance to meet monthly with Michael so she could keep in touch. Her response was that I would first have to retract my accusations against my father.

I was dumbstruck.

In the year since the split, my parents had told all our extended family and friends that I was delusional. Even though Karen was the one who had confronted them, I was blamed for 'brainwashing' her, and their anger was squarely aimed at me. I was slandered and vilified to such an extent that I received a letter from my grandfather lamenting that I had shamed my family by joining a satanic cult. The lies abounded, yet here I was, offering my mother a chance to have a relationship with her only grandson, and she had said 'no.'

It was the only offer I ever made to her.

Sara

My sister Sara is two years older than I am. I can't remember a time when she wasn't my best friend. In our family of eight children, it went like this: My oldest sister Leanne did her own thing; the next four kids – Darlene, Sara, Ryan, and myself – spent most of our free time together; and the three little ones – Dean, Karen, and Nick – were often with our mom.

My little group of four was further divided in two whenever teams were required – Darlene and Ryan; and Sara and myself.

If Sara got to the (double seater) swing in our driveway first, she saved the seat for me. If I had to share a treat, I shared it with her. The same for Darlene and Ryan.

As I grew older, I was the more serious one; Sara the fun one. She brought out the silly in me, and I brought out her more serious side. We were each other's yin and yang.

As I entered my teen years, I admired and envied her beautiful hair, her curvaceous figure, and her flawless skin (she was voted Prom Queen). I was the skinny plain Jane with an unruly, thick mass of hair and a propensity for my skin to break out at any given moment. It's little wonder I was her biggest fan.

We shared a room and bunk beds. I slept on the top bunk; she slept on the bottom. We would stay awake late into the night, talking and laughing. She'd put her feet on the underside of my mattress and push up; I'd hang my head over the side of the bed and freak her out.

We could laugh at nothing and everything. Our parents and siblings would just shake their heads at us in bewilderment. We lived in our own world.

One summer, my mom (who worked at the local library) brought home a "Learn how to type" instruction book. I was thirteen, Sara fifteen. We taught ourselves to type that summer and would often 'air type' whatever dialogue we heard on television. Our family thought we were crazy!

We also taught ourselves basic sign language and infuriated the others when we used it to have entire conversations. That only made us more determined to keep it up!

I didn't care that Sara had a self-centred side to her. I easily overlooked that quality in my unfailing loyalty to her. It would matter later.

We continued our close relationship into adulthood and into parenthood. I was her first daughter's godmother, and she was my son's. Our lives were linked, and we were more grateful than ever for that after the family split.

Karen

Karen is four years younger than I am, and we've never gotten along. She was one of the three 'little ones', and I didn't pay much attention to her. She was sandwiched between two brothers, and they lived in their own world. As Karen got older, she became arrogant and rigid, believing she was always right. Our personalities couldn't have been more different. Karen's had an edge to it. She went through life as if she always had something to prove.

When Karen got married, she made it clear that I wouldn't be in her wedding party. She chose the two sisters who lived out of province. When I expressed my hurt, she dismissively told me that family didn't matter to her. What she was really saying was that I didn't matter to her.

Ironically, one of the chosen sisters was unable to be at her wedding party because she was pregnant and couldn't travel. Karen was now stuck and had to ask me to replace my sister, as we were the same size and the dress had already been purchased. Neither of us was happy with this turn of events, but pressure from our parents kicked in, and I said 'yes.'

Our relationship never really improved, and it was only because of the family split that we were now on the same side of the line.

After many years of trying to conceive again, I was ecstatic to give birth to our daughter Christine. My pregnancy had been healthy, but I was considered high risk due to health concerns and my being over thirty-five.

The most difficult part of my pregnancy was telling our six-year-old that the baby might have to go back to heaven. Every night our family prayed that I would reach thirty-two weeks in my pregnancy, the magical number to give our baby a fighting chance at being born healthy.

Eleven days before my due date, our beautiful, healthy baby girl was born.

My daughter's birth brought such pangs of grief that my parents would never know her, that my brothers and sisters wouldn't be part of her life. They wouldn't get to laugh at her antics, applaud her never-ending songs, or feel pride in her performances on stage.

My estranged family would never get to know the light and joy of my two children, and the knowledge of it was an ache in my heart.

The years that followed were typical of family life. I continued to be a stay-at-home parent, contributed time and effort into coordinating various outreach programs, and ensured that Michael and Christine explored various interests and hobbies.

Mark and I developed cherished friendships with amazing human beings, couples who have a love of family, fun, faith…and food. They are the family of my heart. To this day, our kids will say, "You're welcome to your friend group," as our closest friends are the parents of their closest friends.

We enjoyed many family vacations, both local and abroad, and discovered that the seven-year difference between our children disappeared when those vacations took us to the beaches of the Caribbean.

Treasured memories!

My sister, Sara, once told me that she married her first husband at the age of twenty-two because it was her way out of the house. She admitted that she had never really loved him, and he saw her as his possession. He was controlling and manipulative. To the world, they presented as the perfect couple with the perfect house and their three perfectly planned children – all girls.

She divorced him after almost thirteen years; met and fell in love with Wil, and they got married a few years later. Sara would often say that Wil was the only person who had ever put her first. He was loving and attentive, and he made her happy.

In the summer of '07, Wil was diagnosed with early-onset Alzheimer's, and by the end of the year, he needed to be placed in a home, as Sara worked outside the home, and she couldn't trust him to stay safe.

My sister had already survived a difficult marriage, endured the ups and downs of living with three daughters, and now was faced with this harsh reality.

When our son was five years old (in 1995), we enrolled him in House League soccer as a summer activity. Little did we know that he would go on to excel at being a goalkeeper and continue his post-secondary education on a soccer scholarship at a U.S university.

Sara's youngest daughter Jo was also leaving for the U.S. to do her master's degree in psychology. She also had her oldest daughter Michelle getting married in August. We decided to have a combined celebration dinner with all three sisters and their families, minus the bride-to-be, as she had other commitments.

We were shocked to hear that my niece planned to invite our estranged parents and siblings to her wedding. Sara was very unhappy about this but had been unsuccessful in getting Michelle to change her mind. Although I, too, felt deeply upset and felt like sending my regrets, I knew I had to attend to support Sara. Karen felt no such obligation and made it clear she would not attend.

A major argument ensued with Karen walking out of our home and out of our lives… again.

It didn't end there.

By the end of that disaster, Karen was no longer in our lives, and she had orchestrated a situation that saw my niece Michelle walk away from her mother, her sisters, my family, and myself.

My son had left home, my sister had walked away again, and my niece, blaming her mother and myself for the situation, had also turned her back on us. Sara was devastated at her daughter's desertion and overwhelmed by the demands of her husband's illness.

A painful year.

My family and I learned to live without Michael, and his visits home were filled with anticipation and excitement and tears when he had to return to school. It was a time of 'hellos' and 'goodbyes'.

Our eleven-year-old daughter Christine struggled with her brother's absence, the loss of her aunt and her two daughters, and her cousin Michelle. She began to develop nervous habits and lost her appetite. It took a lot of talking and a lot of reassuring before she found her way through that fog, and I was grateful to have my little girl back.

Ryan

My brother Ryan and I were born in the same year. He was born in January, and I was born in December. That made us eleven months apart, but at school, we were like twins. That meant we were always in the same grade and shared the same friends.

We came from a culture where having a son was cause for great celebration, as he would carry on the family name. There had been three girls before Ryan, so my father felt great pride when he was born.

Ryan and I always got along, and throughout high school, we went to the same parties and dated each other's friends. I gained privileges – later curfews and more social events - because I was with Ryan.

It had been painful for me to see Ryan walk out of my home, along with the rest of my siblings, that fateful evening and our paths had crossed only a few times since the family split. One of those times, he approached me and apologized for everything. I was unprepared for his apology, so I murmured a 'thank you' and quickly left. It was many years later that we re-connected.

I'm not sure what compelled me to contact Ryan. We had been estranged for twenty-one years; however, I had heard, through the grapevine, that life had been difficult for him and his family, and he was now a single dad with two kids, whom I had never met.

I trusted my instincts and reached out. He agreed to meet me at a local coffee shop. The nerves were there, but so was the familiarity. Time flew by, and at the end of our conversation, we both agreed that we wanted to re-establish our relationship and we wanted to have our children meet each other.

This wasn't an easy decision for either of us. For Ryan, it meant facing my father's fury at this 'betrayal.' For me, it meant adjusting to a new reality, one that included family from 'the other side'.

Chapter 5

A few months later, our families met for the first time. Nerves were rampant on both sides, but curiosity won out. The four cousins spent several hours asking and answering questions, and, for me, it was a pivotal moment.

The past had entered my present.

The reactions of my two sisters were opposite. My sister Sara had no interest in re-connecting with Ryan, but Karen did. (Karen had re-entered my life once again.) My new relationship with our brother seemed to create an even greater divide between Sara and me.

For several years, she had become increasingly bitter and distant. Life had handed her several hard blows, and she had been unable to bounce back. Whenever I think of Sara, I think of something Yeats wrote. "Things fall apart; the center cannot hold…"

This seemed especially true for Sara.

My once funny, quirky sister had disappeared; in her place was someone I didn't recognize or, if I'm being honest, I wanted to know. Our phone calls became stilted, and there were times when I dreaded phoning her. Gone were the phone calls where we laughed and planned family get-togethers, where we commiserated over the death of much-loved old movie stars. Gone were the visits where laughter could be heard throughout our homes.

Still, we continued to be in each other's lives, sharing birthdays and holidays.

Having my brother back in my life meant that my sister Darlene knew about it. Every Christmas, my sister Darlene and her family would leave their U.S. home to spend the holidays with my parents and siblings.

This year, Darlene asked Ryan if he thought I'd be interested in meeting with her. It wasn't easy to say 'yes.' When the family split back in the nineties, Darlene's loyalty lay with our mother, and her harsh criticism of me had caused me great pain.

I understood Darlene's need to connect. Our mother was in ill health, and our father was not taking good care of her. Having Darlene and Ryan question his ability to care for our mother placed them on one side of the line, and our dad and other siblings were on the other.

My father, outraged at such disrespect, had instructed his lawyer to send a letter to the two of them, barring them from entering the family home. Again, my other siblings stood with him.

In a moment, Darlene and Ryan were on the other side of the family line – much like I had been twenty-one years earlier.

I agreed to meet.

I suppose I did so because I was deeply committed to my own healing, and I had developed a greater understanding of our family dynamics. From the time he got married and had children, my father had created the rules that we were to obey. When we didn't, we were punished by being exiled. No one was allowed to disagree with him…ever.

I knew how painful it was to flounder without the safety net of family, albeit a dysfunctional one. On a blustery evening between Christmas and New Year, I met my sister Darlene and her husband at the hotel where they were staying.

It felt strange and again familiar. No promises were made, and no one spoke about the past. The overriding concern was for our mother, who seemed to be declining rapidly. It was difficult for me to hear this, as I'd been estranged from her for so long and couldn't even envision her having aged.

The holidays ended, and life went back to being 'normal', but not for long.

Six weeks after meeting Darlene, I received a phone call from Ryan. He was sobbing out the words, "Mom died."

Once again, my world shattered.

Ever since the family split, my sister Sara and I would often talk about what it would be like for us when we heard the news that one of our parents had passed away. We knew we wouldn't be welcome at the funeral and so we decided we would have our own memorial with both our families. This was a conversation we'd had many times over the years.

There are no words to truly convey my shock at hearing my mom had died. My only thought was, "I have to call Sara." I could tell she was in the car when she answered. It turns out she already knew. What I hadn't known was Sara had been visiting my mom in the hospital. She hadn't shared that with me.

She was on the way to see my dad, which was another shock. This was the sister who had stood beside me, who had wholeheartedly believed the accusations against our dad, who had vowed she would never go to the funeral of either parent. When I asked why she was going, she said, "To offer my condolences."

I asked if she'd be coming over to my house afterwards. Her answer was 'no'.

Several things happened with the passing of my mother. My sister Darlene flew home immediately; my brother Ryan drove in from out of town, and my sister Sara entrenched herself in the funeral preparations, aligned with my dad and my estranged siblings.

I didn't know how to make sense of any of it. The two siblings who should have been involved – Darlene and Ryan

– had been ousted, and the sibling who had been ousted years ago was now back in the fold.

I couldn't process any of it. I felt such overwhelming grief at the loss of a mother who had never loved me, had never fought for me, and ultimately had abandoned me. Her death brought up all the years I had yearned for her love; the years of trying to be a good enough daughter; the years of being estranged.

I grieved the harsh reality that I would never see her face again.

My grief was quite different from Darlene's and Ryan's. They grieved the loss of a mother who loved them, who was loving and nurturing, a mother I'd never known.

I decided to go to the funeral Mass. The one thing my mother did give me was the gift of my Christian religion. I felt I owed it to her to be there. Mark went with me, along with Darlene and her husband, Ryan and his two children.

It was a step back in time. There were so many friends and relatives whom I hadn't seen since the family split. I saw my sister Sara with her daughters. They were sitting in the front pew with the rest of the immediate family. That felt like another betrayal.

Before the Mass began, I was approached by a young woman who offered her condolences to me. She was my niece, my youngest brother's daughter. I'd never met her.

She and her younger sister were estranged from their own dad – another fallout from our dysfunctional family - and were there on their own. We immediately invited them to sit with us.

Our group sat at the rear of the church.

My sister Darlene has often said that she doesn't know how she and Ryan would have survived mom's death if it hadn't been for Karen and myself. We provided meals, gatherings at our home, and support. How strange it was to be offering comfort to them for the passing of our mother.

I don't know if it ever occurred to them that I was also grieving.

Sara made no immediate effort to get in touch. She was immersed in the funeral plans, and I felt blindsided by her betrayal.

One week later, she called.

Before my mom's death, we'd been making plans for a family get-together with both families. She began the conversation with questions about the dinner. I was dumbfounded. It was as if nothing had happened, and she'd simply picked up where we'd left off.

I told her that I'd been heartbroken that we hadn't spent the time grieving together and reminded her of the plan we'd always made. She dismissed it by saying, "Things change," among other comments, and ended by stating that I had not done anything to help her with Wil for the past seven years (the length of time he'd been in a home).

I was numb with shock. I had done my very best to stand beside Sara during this horrible time in her life, and the entire time, she had been holding back feelings of anger and resentment that I hadn't been there for her.

After some vicious emails from Sara's daughter Michelle (who'd recently reconciled with her mother) and a bitter letter from Sara, she (along with her daughters) walked out of my life and my family's.

I didn't know how to react to any of it – my mother's death, all the unanswered questions I still had, Sara's behavior, her betrayal – all of it swirled in my heart and my head like a sandstorm.

The emotional tsunami continued in the coming months – Mark's company closed its Canadian doors, and he was out of work; a dear friend received a diagnosis of stage four lung cancer; my son got engaged and was planning to return home to save money for the wedding; and my daughter, my baby was gearing up to leave home for college.

The words 'emotional roller coaster' took on a whole new meaning. I worried about our financial future with Mark out of work. I celebrated the joy of Michael's news. I agonized over my friend's diagnosis. I helped Christine prepare for moving into residence. Coating all of that was a film of grief and heartache over my mother's death and my sister's desertion that I gave in to whenever I had a quiet moment.

That summer was a blur of pain and loss, joy, and excitement. By the fall, Mark was in a new job. Michael was back at home, and our daughter Christine had settled into a new rhythm at school.

By the end of the year, we'd lost Sara and her family; we gained Darlene and hers. Ryan and his family were still in our lives, as well as Karen and hers.

Nothing stays the same.

As our excitement over Michael's wedding intensified, my sister Karen called and asked if I would meet her for coffee. My first thought was, *the other shoe's about to drop.* And it did.

Karen is a deeply troubled woman, and I wasn't particularly surprised when she accused me of multiple acts of violence, culminating with 'physically torturing' her the day of her wedding, at our mother's command, over twenty-five years ago.

As I listened to my deeply disturbed sister calmly outlining how I, along with other siblings, did so in ways that left no bruises, a million different emotions ran through me – from shock to absolute disbelief to profound sadness.

When I made it clear to her that the above had never taken place, she got up and walked out of the coffee shop.

Gone again.

It took an even stranger twist when Mark called her the next day to let her know that we would be taking over the bridal shower for Michael's fiancée Marie, which Karen had been eager to host. She was outraged and couldn't understand why she couldn't still host. She was fully prepared to pretend to the guests that all was well between us.

I haven't seen her since, and that day solidified what I'd believed for a long time. My sister's trauma was more than her psyche could deal with, and it broke her. She would often speak of the past where she played a heroic role in her own abuse, sharing how she fought our father, how she caused him so much pain that he had to go to the hospital. At the time, she would have been eight.

My sister has rewritten her past so that she can emerge as a heroic victim, and the result was more loss for my own family. Her two daughters were not allowed to see my children or me. They had been planning to attend Michael's wedding and now were forbidden to do so.

Not much has changed as I conclude this part of my story. My family and I still have a relationship with the 'new sibs' and their families. We have no contact with Sara and her family or with Karen. Karen's daughters, however, have been wonderful about keeping in touch, despite their mother's emotional storm whenever they get together with my family or me.

While my 'lost and found' family is often a source of upheaval, I'm thankful every single day for Mark and our children, who bring joy to my life.

They are the light to all that is dark.

Chapter 6

"To have faith is to have wings." (J.M. Barrie)

My mother was Catholic, and my father wasn't. When they decided to get married, they needed special permission from Rome to do so, with the understanding that all children would be raised in the Catholic faith. Going to Mass was not optional or open for discussion. We simply went.

As a young child, it seemed to me that the walk to church was an eternity. Realistically, it might have been a fifteen-minute walk. I never really minded going to church, as I was curious about Jesus. Our priest would speak about Jesus being present in our midst, and I kept hoping I'd catch a glimpse of Him. I didn't, and I felt as if I was the only one who couldn't see Him.

It didn't stop me from singing all the hymns, though. I loved singing and loved the sound of my voice. Whenever I got a turn on the swing at our house, I would swing as high as I could, singing the hymns we learned at church.

It would occur to me, years later, how painfully ironic it was that there were many times when my dad hurt me on Saturday night, and my mom would wake me up the next morning to attend Mass. Even when she knew it was happening.

When we moved to Canada, Mass continued to be a necessary weekly obligation in our home. All religious holidays were strictly observed.

We went to Midnight Mass on Christmas Eve, fasted on Ash Wednesday, abstained from meat on Lenten Fridays, and, during Good Friday, we weren't allowed to watch TV, listen to the radio, or go out with friends. I remember my mother slapping me one Good Friday because I had put on a red sweater. Didn't I know that I was being disrespectful to Jesus for wearing a sweater the color of blood?

When I was about fourteen, my sister, Sara sent away for a Good News Bible. She had seen an ad on TV from an evangelical show offering free Bibles. I suppose she had started exploring her faith and since we shared a room, we had many conversations about what we believed and didn't. As I read passages from her Bible, I felt drawn in. Jesus' words resonated. So, I sent away for my own. (Decades later, I still have it.)

I found the Bible comforting. When my parents argued, when my mother threatened to leave my dad because he was unfaithful again, and when fights took place among the siblings, I would read the passages that spoke of God's love for everyone.

I desperately needed to believe that someone loved me.

At sixteen, I began dating one of my brother Ryan's friends. William was handsome, confident, and easy-going. We dated for just over a year, and I can remember exactly where I was the first time he told me he loved me. My tender, sixteen-year-old heart trembled at the words. No one had ever said those words to me before, not even my parents.

My life was perfect. I loved and was loved in return.

Just after my seventeenth birthday, William broke up with me, and that once-trembling heart was now shattered. I didn't know where to turn. Family, friends – no one could understand my crippling pain. What should have been a typical teenage breakup morphed into a near nervous breakdown. Such was the grief of losing the one person who had shown me love.

In my desperation, I found myself going to Mass every evening just so I could have a quiet place to grieve. There, I began to feel a sense of calm. There, I heard the words repeated, "God loves you."

My faith became a priority, and Mass my sanctuary. I leaned on both heavily in those early days, weeks, and months after William, and slowly, I became stronger and steadier. This was a solitary experience, as my family couldn't understand my extreme reaction to the breakup. How could I explain the pain, the devastating sense of loss when I didn't fully understand it myself?

Already, they saw me as different.

I didn't look like either parent, and there were often jokes among the siblings that I must have been adopted. When my parents began to make new friendships in Canada, and those friends came to visit, the eight of us were always instructed to line up, youngest to oldest. Each child was then introduced. I was often described as the different one.

As a young teen, I would sit in my room and write my thoughts and feelings down. There were so many feelings! Sometimes those notes would be found and read out loud to much laughter and to my deep embarrassment. I remember crying one Remembrance Day at the thought of all those lives lost, and my parents were completely baffled by that. Why would I be sad about that when so many people were dying every day? I could hear their laughter as I lay in my bed.

It's little wonder I shared nothing with my parents.

As time passed, my faith became a part of me, and I couldn't imagine my life without it. When I began to date Mark, I was thrilled to discover that we shared the same faith. It certainly made life easier when we decided to get married. Mark also had a strong faith, and as newlyweds, we became quite involved in various programs at our church.

Those early years laid a faith foundation that would be a lifeline for me later.

Chapter 7

It hurts to remember...

It took the family argument over my father's retirement party to make me finally, finally realize that nothing I did was ever going to make my mother love me. I was repeatedly told that all my efforts were seen as 'only to be expected'.

That first craniosacral treatment I received from Alice opened a door for me that had been locked for a lifetime. As I continued those treatments, I understood that the pain I'd been feeling in my body related directly to the pain I'd experienced as a child. I'd been holding on to that pain all my life.

My therapy sessions with Kate allowed me to clearly see for the first time how the family we presented to the outside world was nothing at all like the family we really were. With Kate, I could step back and explore the difference between the truth and the illusion.

This trifecta of awareness came together to create the perfect storm that led to the unraveling of my life as I knew it. Without warning, I found myself on a tumultuous path of horrific memories, excruciating pain, insightful awareness, and transformative healing.

Little did I know at the time that my desperate need to write down my experiences would lead to the writing of my story. With the aid of my journals, I share with you a glimpse into those hurting times…

(After a craniosacral session with Alice)

I walked back to work, feeling unable to move my feet. It was as if my body was shutting down. I don't even remember reaching my desk. Then came the feeling of such sadness and aloneness. My whole body was shaking, and then I had an image of a little girl, and I knew she was me, a child with hair draped over one side of her face. She was stooped over so low to the ground as if there were an enormous weight on her shoulders…the feelings and questions on her face – betrayal, sadness, pain, such pain – not knowing what she'd done to deserve this pain….

The image of this small child stayed with me the rest of the day and night. I needed Mark to pick me up from work, as my limbs felt heavy and numb. By the time we got home, I was running a fever of 103 F – on the hottest day of July.

(One evening, Mark and I went shopping for a

new mattress)

Next to the one we chose, there was a blue mattress. I felt vaguely disturbed seeing it. Later that night, I found myself crying, and I tell Mark:

"I'm five, and I don't like that blue mattress. Don't make me go on that mattress. Not like my daddy. Daddy, why are you doing this? Please don't do this. I don't like it. It hurts."

I'm crying so hard. Inside my head, I'm screaming. I'm in shock. Mark's face shows shock too. We're in something uglier than my worst nightmare. I can take anything else, but not this. Not my dad.

I understood then the image of that small child and why she was so stooped over. She had been carrying the pain and shame of the abuse for a very long time, and it was more than she could bear.

Over many weeks, the regressions continued. My sister Sara, Kate, Alice, and Mark were the only ones I could confide in. The memories came crashing in, wave after wave. Mark and I held on to Kate's reassurance that what I was experiencing wasn't some sort of breakdown; but rather the result of no longer being able to hold back those repressed memories. Kate was our lifeline. She listened, she reassured us, she offered support, and most importantly, she gave us hope.

I never once thought I was going crazy, even though there were times I felt it. I knew what I was remembering was true because there were so many memories that I'd held all my life that made no sense, and now they did.

When I asked Sara if we'd ever had a mattress in a back room in our old house, she said yes, a blue one. Having Sara confirm that memory and many others gave me such strength.

I don't know how Mark knew instinctively to engage with this little girl. He would come down to her eye level so as not to hover over her. He spoke quietly and said all the right things. She felt safe and able to use her voice:

There were times when I refused to believe it was my dad who was hurting me, and the voice of this little girl would emerge:

After many desperate and frantic attempts to deny the truth, I had to accept that it was indeed my father who had hurt me. The pain was unbearable. Some part of me had created a fantasy dad who was perfect, while I thought of my perpetrator as a monster. Saying goodbye to my perfect dad was gut-wrenching. I was left with a monster.

Life was unpredictable during this period of regressions. I would alternate between my adult self and my child self. It felt as if I had one foot in my adult reality and the other in my childhood. Straddling both worlds was exhausting and unnerving.

So many tears were shed as I relived the nightmare that was my childhood. I saw clearly how parts of myself went into hiding, simply to survive, like this one. She called herself 'the one who died.'

I can't stand the pain. I'm dead now, but I'll have to pretend that I'm alive. I'm so angry that he killed me inside. I feel so old, like a shriveled old woman, and my eyes burn with the awful knowing...

Why didn't anyone help me? I had to just leave. I didn't know where to go, and I was so scared. I've been out in the dark for such a long time...

Mark's voice was gentle as he told her that this was where her journey brought her. He invited her to stay with him, so that he could take care of her.

When I returned to my adult self, I was utterly distraught and unable to deal with her crushing pain. I was inconsolable, and for the first time, the thought of ending my life came into my consciousness. I thought of the pills in the medicine cabinet; I thought of how easy it would be to just walk out into the middle of the road and wait for it to be over. Those thoughts were shocking, and in desperation, I took down my framed picture of the Sacred Heart of Jesus, leaned it against the wall, and lay my head on His Heart, weeping. The only words I could muster were, "Lord, help me." Within moments, I could breathe again.

Life, as we knew it, continued. The summer was upon us, and Mark was on vacation for two weeks. On our first day of the holidays, we decided to have lunch downtown because Mark had an afternoon appointment. I agreed to wait for him, and we would head home together. His appointment went much longer, and by the time we met, I was exhausted. I wasn't used to being out of the house for such a long time. The longer I waited, the more enraged I became.

Once we were home, I began pacing in our living room:

I'm the one who hates.... You're all the same, all you men, you only care about yourselves. I didn't ask for this. All of you, you forced the hate down my throat. You chained me to it.... All you care about is what you want. What does it matter if someone hurts that little five-year-old? Or the seven-year-old? It's my job to look out for them. I have to be tough. I hate all men...

The hatred, the disgust, brought Mark to tears. It was impossible for him not to take it personally, and my adult self was terrified that he would break and I would have been responsible.

Thankfully, Mark recognized that this child felt she had to protect the other girls; while the girls felt pain, she held the anger and hatred for what had been done to them.

Mark: I understand why you feel that way, but I still love you.

Me: Why do you want to love me? I'm nothing to you.

Mark: I love you, just like I love all the other girls. It's all right if you don't love me back.

Me: You know, the hate's not inside me. I just have to carry it. It's my job to look out for the girls.

Mark: Well, you can visit or stay here with the girls. Maybe you can just put down the hate. You don't need it anymore. You're safe here.

Me: Maybe I'll stick around for a while...it's been lonely...

There are many, many more entries in my journal that speak to the heart-wrenching memories of having been violated by my father and, to a much lesser degree, two male friends of the family. Putting them all down on paper serves little purpose. It's enough to know that they happened.

As did this:

I'm exhausted after this last girl. I can't stop crying. Mark just holds me and lets me cry. I can't explain how I feel. Raw and open, as if someone has unwrapped my bandages and left the tender skin open to the air. Everything hurts. The tender skin is all of me. I feel everything, and there is such a profound knowing when these words are uttered from a place deep within me:

"I am light. I am goodness and truth. I am life and love. I am one with God, and He is one with me."

I feel indescribable joy, love, and serenity. I feel God's presence as if the veil that separates heaven and earth has been ever so slightly pulled back. And these are the words that are imprinted in my mind and on my heart:

"I came because you entered your pain, seeking truth and light. When you rested your head against my heart, I wept with you."

After a while, I find myself quieting down and sitting on the floor of our living room. In my heart and mind, the words continue:

"Whenever you look inside to the light, you will find Me always."

Chapter 8

The Things I've Learned...

When Mark and I got married, we had no idea our lives would be turned upside down by the experiences I've shared. I am grateful we didn't know.

Without a doubt, our marriage was greatly affected by my trauma and the work around it. There were times when Mark felt overwhelmed and needed to escape, times when I didn't want to be touched, and times when we clung to each other like survivors on a raft, tossed around on a stormy sea.

We emerged from that time in our lives bruised and battered, and we had to work hard to create some semblance of normal, not just for ourselves but also for our children.

For me, that was the easy part. I loved parenting and found myself getting stronger and more confident caring for Michael and Christine. They grounded me and healed me in ways beyond anything I could have imagined.

After that experience at the sandbox, I was able to use my voice to advocate for Michael, something I would never have done for myself. There was no stopping me after that. My children knew that I would stand for them, protect them, and heaven help anyone who tried to hurt them!

My faith continued to grow, and my strong spiritual connection opened the door for further extraordinary experiences that both challenged and inspired me. As time went on, it became harder and harder to open myself to those experiences while trying to live every day, and so I closed that door. I needed to feel grounded, and I simply wanted to be with my family.

The years spent at home with the kids also allowed me an opportunity to get to know myself. I recognized my passion for community outreach and for helping organizations that focused on the helpless as a result of my own feelings of being powerless. I directed my energy to projects that empowered and educate others.

With time I came to better understand the complex dynamics that governed my birth family. I truly believe that my father's personality held traits of narcissism, and my mother was drawn into a dark and destructive relationship with him. What remains a painful mystery to me is why she chose to stay with him, why she chose to stand with him instead of standing with her children.

The invisible thread that connected us all was woven out of fear and denial.

By choosing a different path, I had cut that thread and disrespected my father, his rules, and his vision of the perfect family. It took me such a long time to truly accept that I wasn't the one lacking. That lack existed in my parents, who lived with their own demons and were unable to provide a healthy, affirming love.

I grieved the loss of my family even as I understood that it was the only way I could grow in my new life.

I learned that the past may not have defined me, but it played a critical role in how I defined myself. I had seen myself as bad, unlovable, less than others…unworthy.

I realized that I had tried desperately to compensate for all my perceived failings by trying so hard to be 'good.' I was everyone's friend. I made myself available to family and friends whenever they needed me. They mattered more than I did.

I often say to other survivors that working on my healing felt like being the lone survivor of an emotional earthquake. I was left standing amidst the rubble of my old life that had been broken into pieces, and I had to sift through all of it to find the pieces I wanted to keep. The pieces of myself that I needed in order to rebuild my life.

There were so many pieces of that old life that were never mine. I was pregnant with Michael when the piece marked SHAME slammed into my consciousness. Its power was crippling.

Help came in the form of two people who were recommended by Dr. H., my family doctor. They were a husband-and-wife team who practiced Rei Ki, something I'd never heard of. While I was skeptical, I was also willing to seek help wherever I could find it.

With some trepidation, I scheduled an appointment. Within minutes of meeting Al and Doreen, I experienced the warmth of two gentle souls who offered a safe space for me to continue my healing.

I remember sharing the feeling of the weight of that shame smothering me, and these two dear people lovingly, emphatically stating that the shame never belonged to me. It belonged to my father, even though I was the one carrying it around in an invisible backpack. And then they asked if I could simply put the backpack down and choose to no longer carry it. It was another pivotal moment.

I've never picked that backpack up again.

I learned that I needed to acknowledge my anger, another piece that terrified me. It had always been easier to feel sadness, confusion, and despair. I didn't want to connect with my anger because I knew that it was huge and, once acknowledged, would overpower me like my father.

Again, it was Al and Doreen who walked this part of the journey with me.

Whenever they brought up the topic of anger, I would always say it was too huge to tackle. I would need to have a big space to unleash my anger, such was its enormity.

Well, they took me literally and called me one day to say they had a friend's empty dance studio at their disposal one evening. They were definitely on a mission to help me free myself from my anger. With much anxiety, I agreed to meet them at the studio with Mark.

We secured a babysitter for Michael and walked out of our home, with me carrying a pillow. I imagined Mark holding the pillow while I punched it a few times. That didn't happen!

We arrived at the studio on a rainy evening. Mark was meeting Al and Doreen for the first time. Imagine that introduction! As we entered the room, I noticed that Doreen had brought a CD player. She turned it on, and the room was filled with the sound of drumming.

Can you imagine how silly I felt, standing in the middle of this empty room while three people waited for me to do something, anything? Earlier, I had instructed Mark to read excerpts from my journals that had to do with my dad and to keep repeating them. I believed it would help me connect to my anger.

I felt so foolish as Mark held the pillow and began repeating phrases from my journal, but I had to start somewhere. Timidly, I began to punch the pillow, and then I don't really know what happened. Perhaps it was the drumming in the background or the words coming out of Mark's mouth; whatever it was, I began hitting the pillow so hard I was pushing my 6'5" husband off his feet.

At one point, Al (6'3") had to stand behind Mark to anchor him as I continued to punch, swear, and scream out all the anger I had buried deep inside my body. There was so much rage. How had I lived all those years with that poison inside my body?

It seemed like an eternity before I lay on that empty floor, drenched in sweat and beyond exhaustion. In some strange way, it felt as if I'd gone through a birthing experience, only this time I wasn't pushing out a child. I was expelling an enormous amount of rage.

When Mark asked me how I felt, the first words out of my mouth were, "I'm starving!" Everyone laughed, and we ended that strange night sharing a meal at a restaurant.

Once I had rid myself of the shame that had weighed me down and the anger that had filled me up, I felt free. I was free to be me, whoever that was. I became more confident and less needy.

I discovered that I could be my own safe place.

As the work had taken a toll on our marriage, in a less spectacular way, so did my transformation. Mark had become accustomed to being my rock, my advocate, and now, I was standing solidly on my own two feet. He was left feeling confused about his role in our relationship.

It took time, commitment, and effort for us to create a new dynamic, a healthier one that created space for us to be individuals as well as a couple. The new normal came with lots of confusion about expectations and needs being met or ignored. We weathered that storm because we knew the love between us was strong, even during those times when we didn't feel it.

I've learned to pay close attention to my feelings and express them when I need to. I no longer believe that others are more worthy than I am. I am worthy of being loved and seen and heard and understood.

I needed to allow those memories to surface, to give voice to them and let them go. By shining a light into those dark places, I could finally face the monster, knowing I was no longer that scared little girl.

I've often felt that I've climbed mountains and traveled a million miles… all in my heart, my mind, my soul. That's been the journey I unknowingly embarked on in my search for truth.

There is one aspect of my trauma that can still rear its ugly head… fear. If shame was the backpack and anger was the enormous 'thing' I carried inside of me, fear was the cloak I wore.

Each time one of those little girls appeared, her first words were usually, "I'm scared."

There was no pivotal moment in my healing journey where I conquered fear. It lessened each time one of the girls shared her story and was reassured that she was safe.

From those experiences, I recognized one of my core beliefs: Fear keeps me feeling unsafe.

I feel no shame in sharing that I cannot sleep in complete darkness. I need to be able to see the doorway of our bedroom. Thankfully, there are no objections from Mark, even when we have to take a nightlight with us on vacation.

I've learned that fear is like any other emotion. If I feed it, it becomes stronger. For my fear to lessen, I have to ask myself, "Is this an old fear?" If it is, I can reassure myself that I'm no longer that little child, remind myself of all that's good in my life, and that reassurance allows my fear to fade.

Of course, there are always going to be things that I'm afraid of. The smaller ones I try to tackle and the bigger ones I give to God to manage.

We are living with the challenges of Covid as we near the end of this year, and another age-old belief has surfaced because of the danger and uncertainty of this virus: 'the unknown is unsafe.' As a child, this belief was a painful reality and one I thought I'd exorcised. It turns out I hadn't.

The reality of Covid brings up old feelings of being helpless, powerless, and afraid, and that is a poignant reminder to me that I am not, nor will I ever be, completely healed of my trauma.

There are moments in my everyday reality that take me traveling back in time to those dark and painful childhood experiences, and I've learned to accept that. I do so, knowing that I am no longer helpless or powerless.

With all my heart, I believe that vulnerability speaks to courage and gentleness to strength. I choose to use those qualities to gain insight and understanding whenever I'm triggered by old memories.

I recognize that while my wounds may have healed, there are many scars, and I'm not ashamed of them. They are the marks of a warrior.

Chapter 9

For you who are hurting…

If you are reading this book and are a victim of childhood abuse of any kind, the first thing I'd like to say is how sorry I am that it happened. I'm sorry that you're in pain.

You didn't deserve to be hurt. You did nothing wrong. You are not to blame.

Whatever your situation, I hope and pray that you have someone in your life whom you trust. I know trust is hard. I also know healing cannot happen alone. If there is no one, please reach out to an organization that serves victims of abuse. The first step is the hardest.

A child's birthright is to be loved and protected by the adults in their life. When those adults fail the child, the fault lies with them. It is not the child's fault. It is not your fault.

So often, I hear from other survivors that their lives were ruined by the abuse. It saddens me to hear this because I hear the truth in their words. I hope you can hear the truth in mine. It doesn't have to be that way.

Once I stopped hiding from the pain and the shame, I found the strength to keep going. There were times when those feelings had me buckling at the knees. What kept me going was my need to know what was true. So much of my childhood and my family life was a lie.

You are more than your abuse. Yes, it takes up a lot of space, and it can sometimes feel like there's room for nothing else. I encourage you to think about other aspects of your life. Take a few steps back and look at every day of your life.

Are there areas of that life that make you proud, that satisfy? If there's even one, it's because you were able to create space for something good, something worthwhile.

Imagine what it would be like if you could clear out all those dark and hurting places inside of you. Imagine the freedom of choosing how to fill that space!

There is so much more to who you are than something that happened to you. There were times when I wanted to give up, to simply crawl back into the pit of shame and denial. Whenever that happened, I thought to myself, *No way am I going to let him win. He's not going to ruin the rest of my life!*

In other words, my greatest revenge was to create a full and meaningful life.

As survivors, we know better than most how the darkness can take over all that's good in our lives, so I encourage you to actively seek out joyful moments. Joy is everywhere!

I find it in the noisy fun of family dinners, gathering with friends for a meal, the beauty of a song, and quiet time with a good book. When I look out my bedroom window and see the cardinals at the bird feeder, I'm filled with delight. They bring such vibrant color to a dreary winter day.

The kitchen in our home has a sign that says, "My kitchen is for dancing." I received that from a friend who knows that I love to put on music while I'm cooking and often end up dancing to some infectious tune. Anyone who crosses my path must join in! Dancing makes me happy.

You might be thinking, "I can't; I just can't talk about what happened." I gently ask, "Who can't? Is it the little child who felt powerless, helpless? The child who took on the blame, the shame?"

I believe in you, and I believe you can. Not talking about your abuse is about keeping a secret. You don't have to be quiet any longer. You have the right to use your voice to tell your story.

The famous author and poet Ralph Waldo Emerson sums it up perfectly:

"What lies behind us and what lies before us are but tiny matters compared to what lies within us."

Acknowledgments

My Gratitude...

"At times, our own light goes out and is rekindled by a spark from another person." *(Albert Schweitzer)*

Each morning, I wake up, giving thanks to God for the day and asking Him to help me live it the best way I can.

I know my life could have gone in a different direction, and I'm so grateful that I was able to persevere and create a life that is graced with faith, family, and friends.

There aren't words to convey the joy I feel at being free from the constraints of my past, my childhood, and my abuse.

I could never have done this alone, and it's vital that I convey my gratitude to those who walked with me, who stood with me, and who picked me up whenever I fell.

My guardian angel has always been and continues to be Mark. He believed me from the very beginning, and his belief in me gave me the strength to keep going. He found a way to engage with my girls that gave them permission to speak unspeakable things and offered love, kindness, and reassurance.

I know that Mark paid the price for loving me. He, too, has been on the receiving end of much criticism and anger, yet it didn't weaken his resolve to help me remember and to heal.

He is the best man I know.

My children have been instrumental in my healing. They allowed me to give expression to my own need for love and joy. Wanting to bring a child into our lives was a huge motivator for embarking on the journey, and I think of Michael as my reason. Seven years later, Christine arrived as my reward for staying true and refusing to give up.

I am humbled by my children's love for me. They are fiercely protective and are proud of me that I had the courage to forge my own path so that they could grow up in a loving, safe home.

Together, they add goodness and light to my life, and I am grateful to God every day for them.

My sister Sara had to make a painful choice when she chose me over our family, and I will always be indebted to her. She never doubted me for a second and made the time to call me daily, sometimes more than once, to check in, to let me know that she was there for me. As a wife and busy mom of three children, this caused friction in her own marriage, yet she never wavered.

She once told me that helping me through the trauma was her way of dealing with her own. She was also my resource, being two years older, as she often validated the memories that surfaced.

I miss Sara, the sister I love who possessed a quirky sense of humor and made me laugh. She is in my heart forever.

Our family doctor at the time, Dr. H., was a kind and gentle man. His quiet strength, his belief in me, and his efforts to help me find the right professionals to support me gave me another place to feel safe.

I think of my craniosacral therapist, Alice, as the gatekeeper. With skill and compassion, she helped to release the trauma from my body and opened the door for healing to begin.

Al and Doreen gave me such support and encouragement through their words, their skill with Rei Ki, and their love. They taught me that nothing is impossible. If I can envision it, I can create it.

What an incredible lesson to learn!

I think back to my first impression of Kate and the feeling that she could see right through me. In a way, she could.

She saw in me what I didn't - the courage to seek out the truth and the strength to deal with the consequences. She listened, she encouraged, she offered profound insights, and she cared deeply.

She is the most selfless person I've ever known, with an abundance of wisdom and grace, and my love and gratitude for her are boundless.

Finally, it is from the deepest place within me that I give thanks to the One who never left my side. His love for me shone like a beacon of hope and led me out of the dark and into the light.